Prayers for My Baby Boy

KATIE KENNY PHILLIPS
ILLUSTRATED BY AUDREY JEANNE ROBERTS

HARVEST HOUSE PUBLISHERS
EUGENE, OREGON

Katie Kenny Phillips

is the author of several children's books, including *Today I Feel Like a Jelly Donut*; *God, You Make Me Feel Special*; *Jesus Loves Everybody*; and *Let's Find Joy!* with Shaunti Feldhahn. Katie lives in Atlanta, Georgia, with her husband, five kids, and their ridiculous dogs, Norm and Coco.

Cover and interior design by Nicole Dougherty

This logo is a federally registered trademark of the Hawkins Children's LLC. Harvest House Publishers, Inc., is the exclusive licensee of this trademark.

Prayers for My Baby Boy

Published by Harvest House Publishers
Eugene, Oregon 97408
www.harvesthousepublishers.com

ISBN 978-0-7369-9219-0 (hardcover)

Library of Congress Control Number: 2025937401

Printed in China

25 26 27 28 29 30 31 32 33 / DC / 10 9 8 7 6 5 4 3 2 1

WISDOM

Gracious Father,

Give this child a desire for wisdom that only You can supply. Let him seek it as if it were treasure—precious and valuable and life-giving. You tell us that when we need wisdom, we can ask You and You will not withhold it (James 1:5). Thank You for promising to give him the answers he needs and for instilling this yearning for Your will within his heart.

Amen.

If you need wisdom, ask our generous God, and he will give it to you. He will not rebuke you for asking.

JAMES 1:5

PROTECTION

Heavenly Father,

I lay this beautiful child at Your feet. I love him more than I could ever fathom, and it humbles me to know You love him even more. I also lay down my fear and anxiety over his safety and ask You to protect him all the days of his life. I know he does not need to be afraid because You go before him, walk beside him, and will never fail him or abandon him (Deuteronomy 31:8). Help him to always feel Your presence, even when he is alone. And help me loosen my grip as I trust in Your love and care for him.

Amen.

Do not be afraid or discouraged,
for the LORD will personally
go ahead of you. He will be
with you; he will neither fail
you nor abandon you.

DEUTERONOMY 31:8

Jesus told him, "I am the way, the truth, and the life. No one can come to the Father except through me."

JOHN 14:6

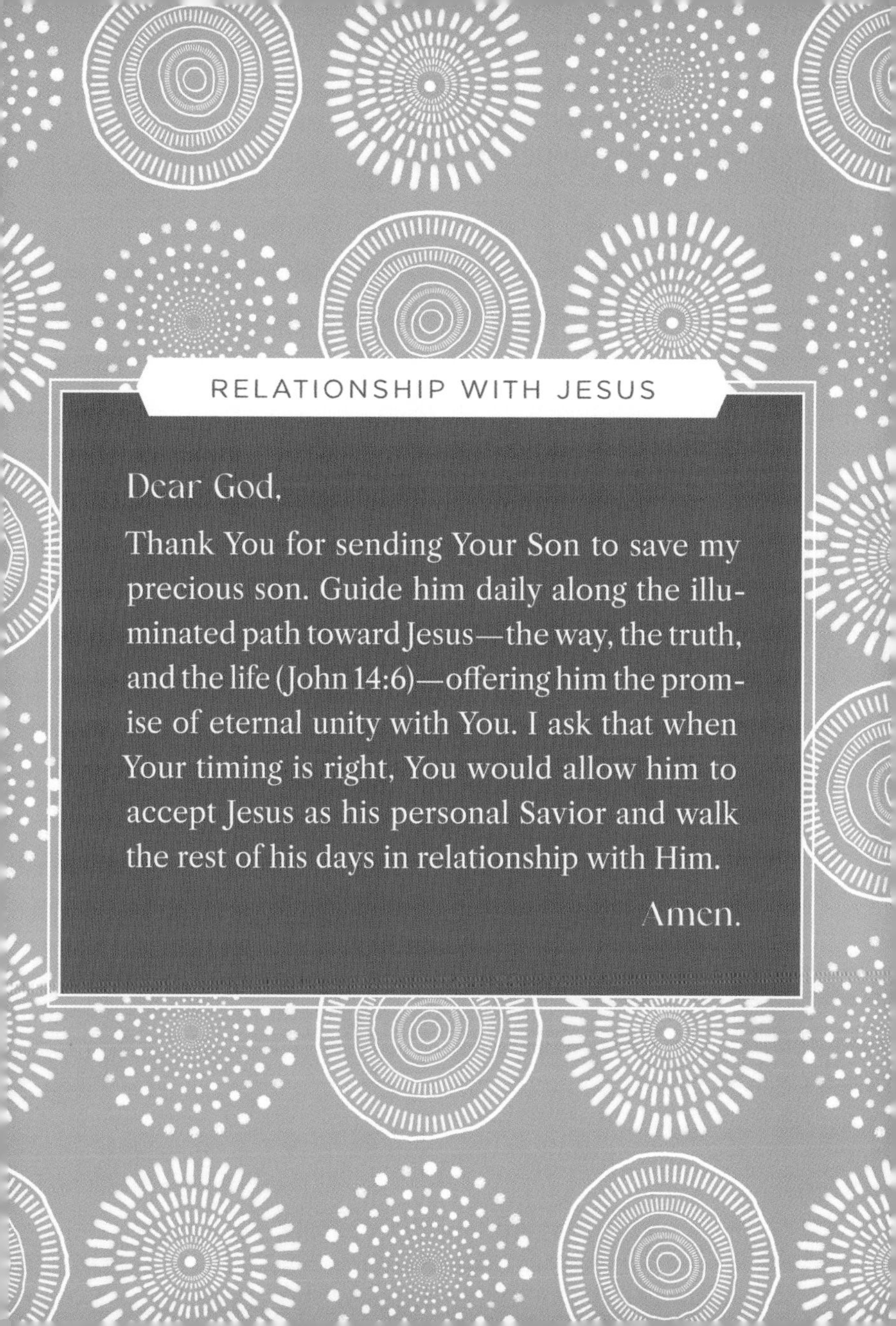

RELATIONSHIP WITH JESUS

Dear God,

Thank You for sending Your Son to save my precious son. Guide him daily along the illuminated path toward Jesus—the way, the truth, and the life (John 14:6)—offering him the promise of eternal unity with You. I ask that when Your timing is right, You would allow him to accept Jesus as his personal Savior and walk the rest of his days in relationship with Him.

Amen.

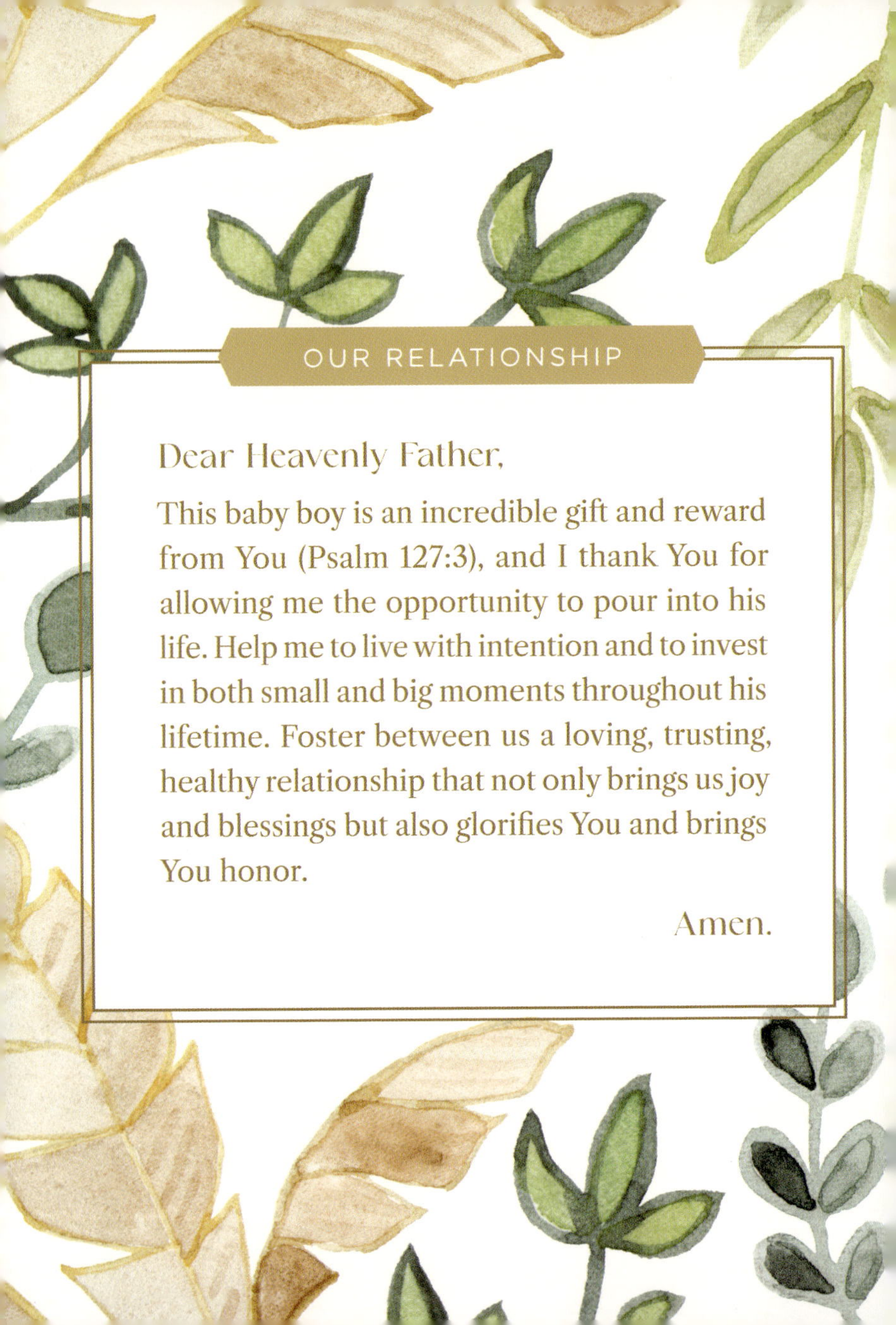

OUR RELATIONSHIP

Dear Heavenly Father,

This baby boy is an incredible gift and reward from You (Psalm 127:3), and I thank You for allowing me the opportunity to pour into his life. Help me to live with intention and to invest in both small and big moments throughout his lifetime. Foster between us a loving, trusting, healthy relationship that not only brings us joy and blessings but also glorifies You and brings You honor.

Amen.

Children are a gift
from the Lord; they are
a reward from him.

PSALM 127:3

A friend is always loyal,
and a brother is born to
help in time of need.

PROVERBS 17:17

SIBLINGS

Dear God,

Bless this baby boy in his relationships with his siblings—both now and in the future. Whether they are within our family or he considers others as close as a sister or brother, grow this baby's heart to bursting with compassion, love, and kindness. Give him the opportunity to not only be loyal but present—noticing, seeing—and a true source of help for his siblings when he is needed most (Proverbs 17:17).

Amen.

COMMUNITY

Dear Father,

Thank You for the community You've prepared for this baby boy throughout his life. I trust You to gather together believers who will love him and be a source of encouragement and strength as he seeks to follow You in this big, beautiful world (Hebrews 10:24-25). May he also have a heart for Your people—serving, comforting, and supporting others as they do the same for him. Make these relationships rich and meaningful—reminders that our relationships are some of Your very best gifts.

Amen.

Let us think of ways to motivate one another to acts of love and good works. And let us not neglect our meeting together, as some people do, but encourage one another, especially now that the day of his return is drawing near.

HEBREWS 10:24-25

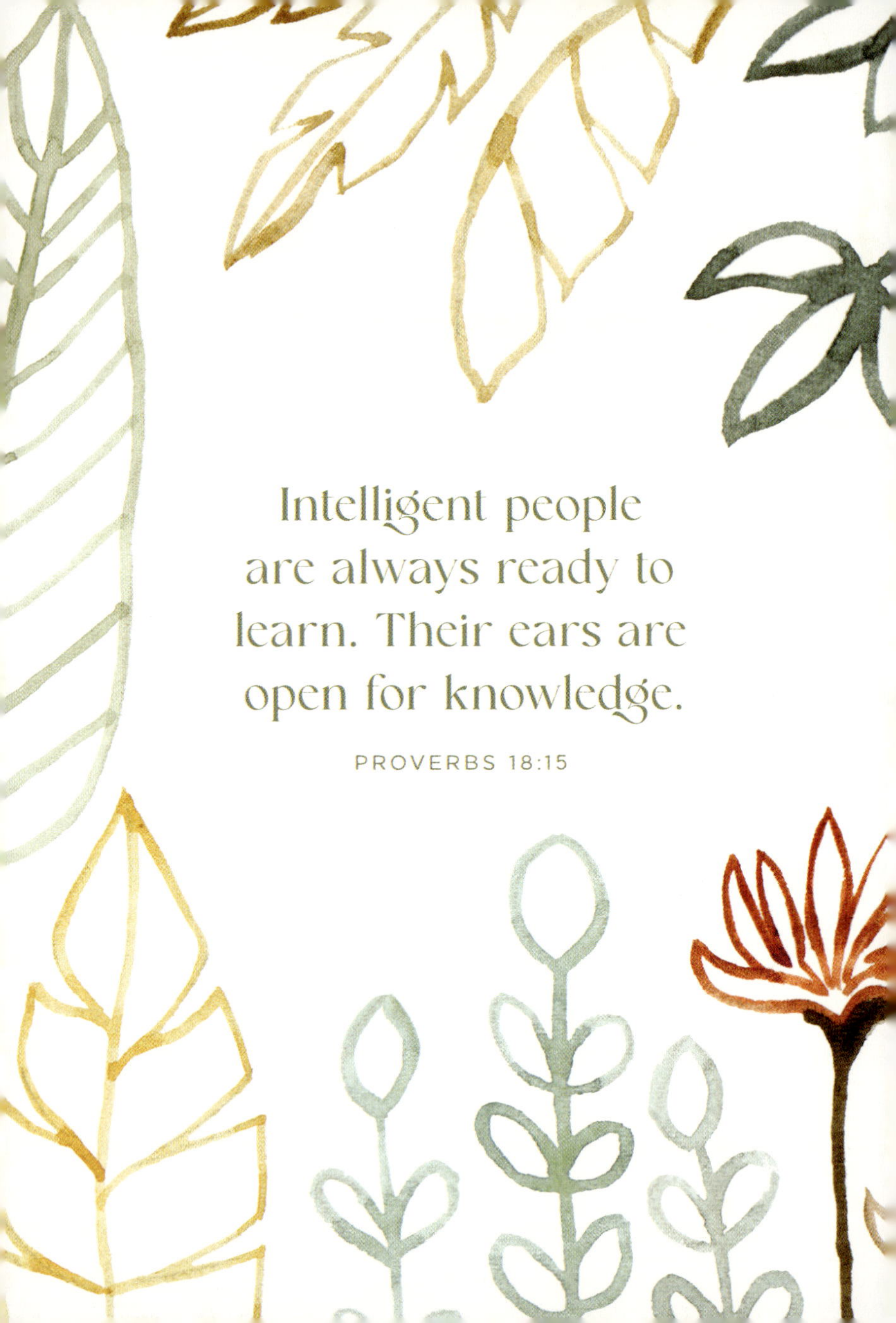

Intelligent people
are always ready to
learn. Their ears are
open for knowledge.

PROVERBS 18:15

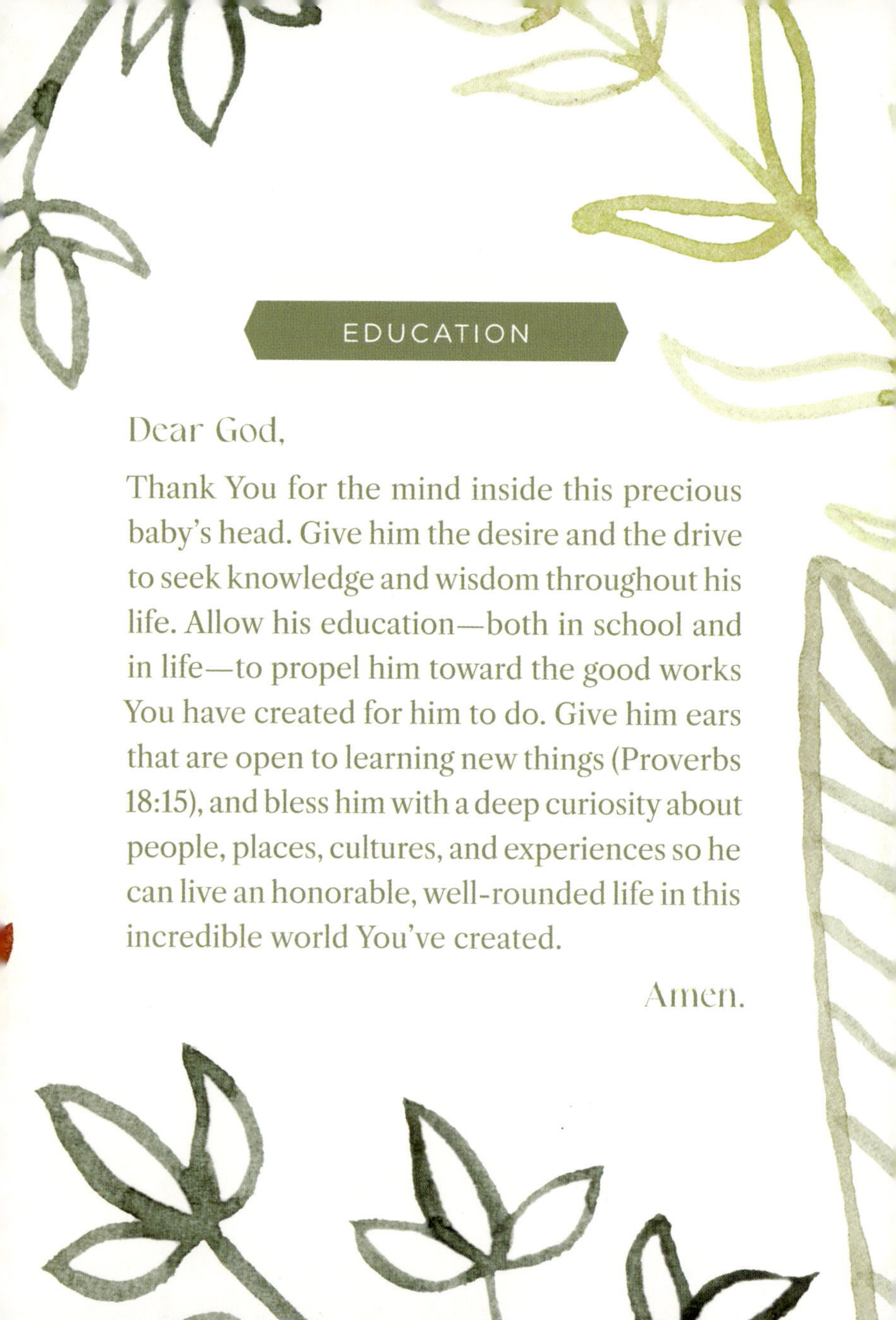

EDUCATION

Dear God,

Thank You for the mind inside this precious baby's head. Give him the desire and the drive to seek knowledge and wisdom throughout his life. Allow his education—both in school and in life—to propel him toward the good works You have created for him to do. Give him ears that are open to learning new things (Proverbs 18:15), and bless him with a deep curiosity about people, places, cultures, and experiences so he can live an honorable, well-rounded life in this incredible world You've created.

Amen.

GENEROSITY

Generous Father,

I pray a spirit of generosity over my son. Give him a soft and compassionate heart to serve others. Open his eyes to those around him. Be a clear and steady voice in his ear so he can hear Your call. Use his life as a way to show others Your goodness, kindness, and mercy. Your Word says that You accept the gifts of Your children, both big and small, when the willingness is there (2 Corinthians 8:12). May his generosity and service be an acceptable gift when he loves others as You do.

Amen.

Whatever you give
is acceptable if you give it
eagerly. And give according
to what you have, not
what you don't have.

2 CORINTHIANS 8:12

Be kind to each other,
tenderhearted, forgiving one
another, just as God through
Christ has forgiven you.

EPHESIANS 4:32

KINDNESS

Kind Father,

Thank You for making this baby boy in Your likeness. I ask that this child radiate Your goodness to the world around him, revealing Your character and drawing people to You. May this sweet soul be kind and tenderhearted to everyone he meets, always remembering to forgive others as You have forgiven us (Ephesians 4:32). When he does this, he will always be an arrow pointing directly to You.

Amen.

VALUE

Loving God,

I have longed for this child—and he is a blessing. Thank You for bringing him into our family—a treasure more valuable than I could have imagined. Please help him know how much he is loved every day of his life—by us, of course, but also by You, his Heavenly Father. May he know deep in his bones that he was adopted into Your family through Jesus Christ and that his existence was created with intention, precision, purpose, and great pleasure (Ephesians 1:5).

Amen.

God decided in advance to adopt us into his own family by bringing us to himself through Jesus Christ. This is what he wanted to do, and it gave him great pleasure.

EPHESIANS 1:5

You love [God] even though
you have never seen him.
Though you do not see
him now, you trust him;
and you rejoice with a
glorious, inexpressible
joy. The reward for
trusting him will be the
salvation of your souls.

1 PETER 1:8-9

JOY

Good Father,

Thank You for the blessing of this baby boy. Please give him eyes to see You, a heart to trust You, and a glorious, inexpressible joy (1 Peter 1:8-9) because You call him Yours. Allow this child to live his life with such overflowing, tangible joy that anyone who comes into contact with him cannot deny You are the source of all that is worthy to be praised.

Amen.

PEACE

Dear God,

You are the giver of good, good gifts, and I praise You for the gift of Your peace. Bless this baby boy with peace of mind and heart—not as the world gives but as only You can (John 14:27). There will be many moments throughout his life that will feel uncertain, but I ask You to pour out Your peace as if anointing him with oil, covering him and marking him as Your own.

Amen.

I am leaving you with a gift—
peace of mind and heart.
And the peace I give is a gift
the world cannot give. So
don't be troubled or afraid.

JOHN 14:27

PATIENCE

Holy God,

You designed this precious baby boy, and his future is full of opportunities to reveal Your glory to others through his actions, words, and prayers. Allow him to hear Your voice when You call him and to work with endurance, and give him the strength to not grow tired of doing good, as it will reap blessings (Galatians 6:9). Help him see the value in planting seeds, watering them, and harvesting based on Your will—and to be patient enough to wait on Your perfect timing.

Amen.

Let's not get tired of doing what is good. At just the right time we will reap a harvest of blessing if we don't give up.

GALATIANS 6:9

Faith shows the reality
of what we hope for;
it is the evidence of
things we cannot see.

HEBREWS 11:1

FAITHFULNESS

Good Father,

I ask that You draw this baby boy into Yourself from his earliest days and make his heart beat for You. When life becomes challenging, please give him the steadfastness and faithfulness to trust in Jesus, even on days and on paths that seem difficult. While he cannot see You, may he feel You beside him as if You are holding his hand (Hebrews 11:1). As the two of you walk together, Your presence will increase and bolster his faith on whatever journey You are guiding him along.

Amen.

GENTLENESS

Gentle Father,

As I hold this child and gently rock him, I know full well You are holding him in Your arms as well. Give him a spirit of gentleness with others, allowing people to feel cared for and understood whenever they are in his presence. Make people stop in wonder at his kindness, and when they spend time with him, give them a sense of Your life-light burning quietly and humbly inside him (Ephesians 4:2).

Amen.

Always be humble and gentle.
Be patient with each other,
making allowance for each other's
faults because of your love.

EPHESIANS 4:2

God has not given us
a spirit of fear and
timidity, but of power,
love, and self-discipline.

2 TIMOTHY 1:7

SELF-CONTROL

Dear God,

There are so many amazing opportunities and experiences ahead for this child. So many people to meet, places to travel, things to learn, and ideas to explore. Will You give him the wisdom and self-control to go forth into this world without fear but with Your power and love (2 Timothy 1:7)? Help him know each step he should take and what he should avoid, and allow him to trust in the communication You will share. Be clear in Your instructions to him, and in that clarity, his self-control will grow stronger every day.

Amen.

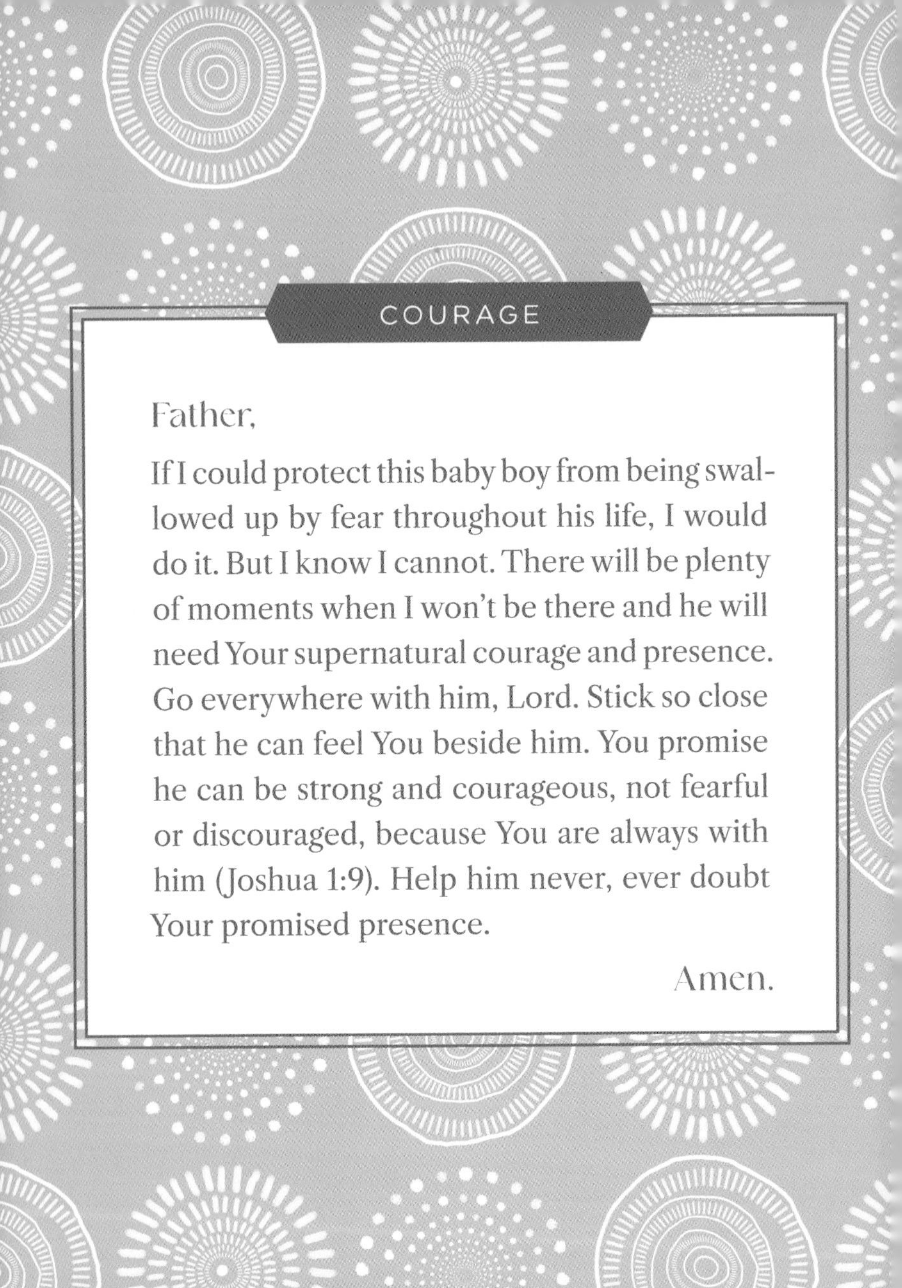

COURAGE

Father,

If I could protect this baby boy from being swallowed up by fear throughout his life, I would do it. But I know I cannot. There will be plenty of moments when I won't be there and he will need Your supernatural courage and presence. Go everywhere with him, Lord. Stick so close that he can feel You beside him. You promise he can be strong and courageous, not fearful or discouraged, because You are always with him (Joshua 1:9). Help him never, ever doubt Your promised presence.

Amen.

This is my command—be strong and courageous! Do not be afraid or discouraged. For the LORD your God is with you wherever you go.

JOSHUA 1:9

This is the day the LORD has made. We will rejoice and be glad in it.

PSALM 118:24

CURIOSITY

Dear God,

This is the day You have made, and I thank You for the reminder that we can always rejoice and be glad in it (Psalm 118:24)! Give this baby boy the desire to seek out joy in the midst of hardship, gratitude in the midst of the mundane, and blessings in the midst of the ordinary. Will You allow him to be curious enough to see Your goodness every day, regardless of his circumstances? Help him fight the culture of negativity and be a noticer of all Your praiseworthy things.

Amen.

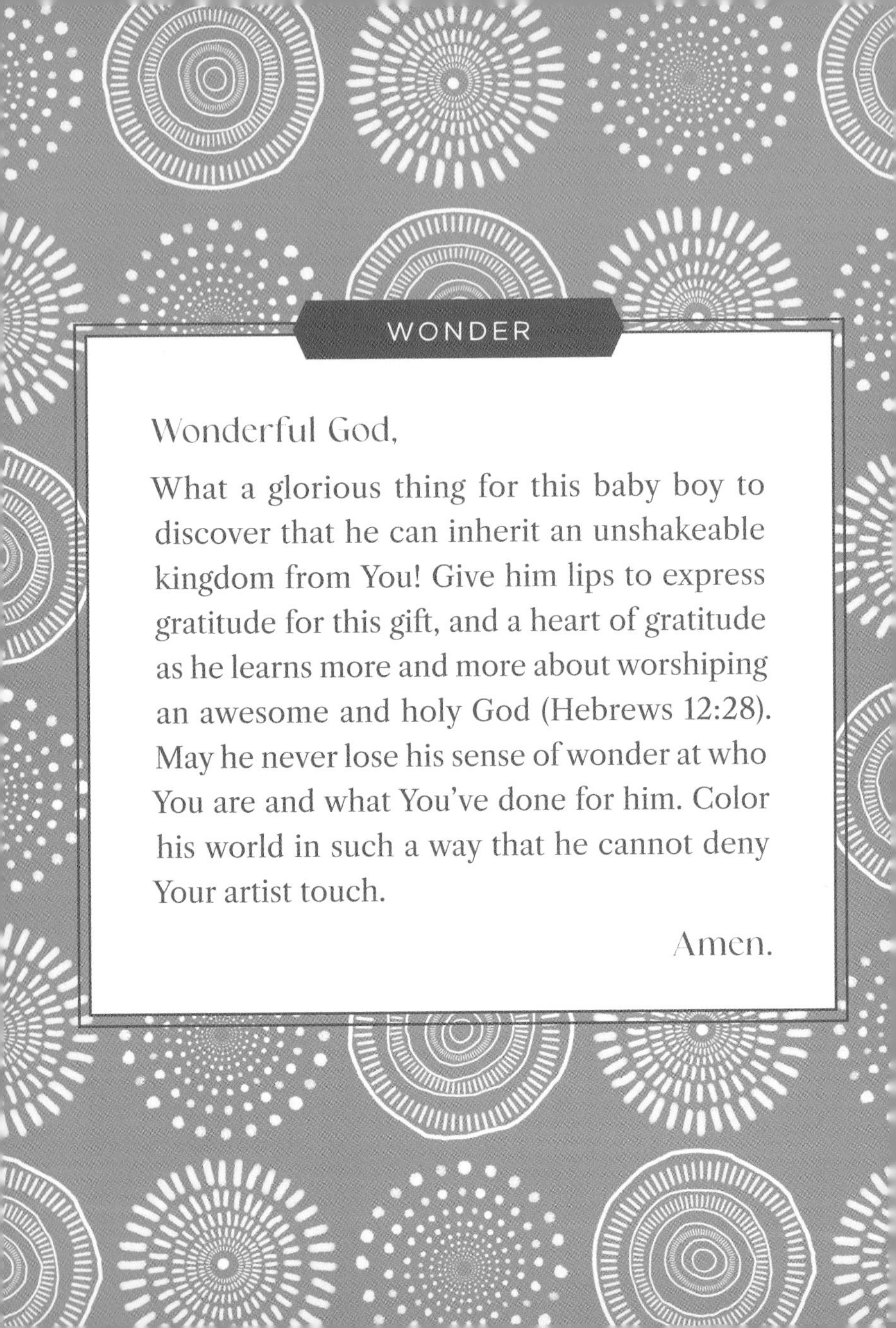

WONDER

Wonderful God,

What a glorious thing for this baby boy to discover that he can inherit an unshakeable kingdom from You! Give him lips to express gratitude for this gift, and a heart of gratitude as he learns more and more about worshiping an awesome and holy God (Hebrews 12:28). May he never lose his sense of wonder at who You are and what You've done for him. Color his world in such a way that he cannot deny Your artist touch.

Amen.

Since we are receiving a
Kingdom that is unshakable,
let us be thankful and please
God by worshiping him
with holy fear and awe.

HEBREWS 12:28

Be thankful in all circumstances, for this is God's will for you who belong to Christ Jesus.

1 THESSALONIANS 5:18

Gracious God,

Give this little boy the desire to plant seeds of gratitude along the winding pathway of his life. His moments will be filled with ups and downs, good and bad, the easy and the difficult, but with Your help he can trust You and give You thanks for each circumstance (1 Thessalonians 5:18). As he matures, I pray he sees a bountiful harvest of blessings, proving that belonging to Jesus results in a fruitful and heart-filled life.

Amen.

WORK ETHIC

Dear God,

I ask that You give this child the desire to work hard and willingly at whatever he does and to commit his work to You (Colossians 3:23). In a world that values shortcuts and quick fixes, may he do what needs to be done to the best of his ability—especially when no one is looking. Let him feel the satisfaction of a job well done and inspire others with his commitment to integrity and excellence. Whatever he chooses to do—from his daily tasks to opportunities to serve others to his future occupation—let his actions always be a sweet, fragrant offering to You.

Amen.

Work willingly at
whatever you do, as
though you were
working for the Lord
rather than for people.

COLOSSIANS 3:23

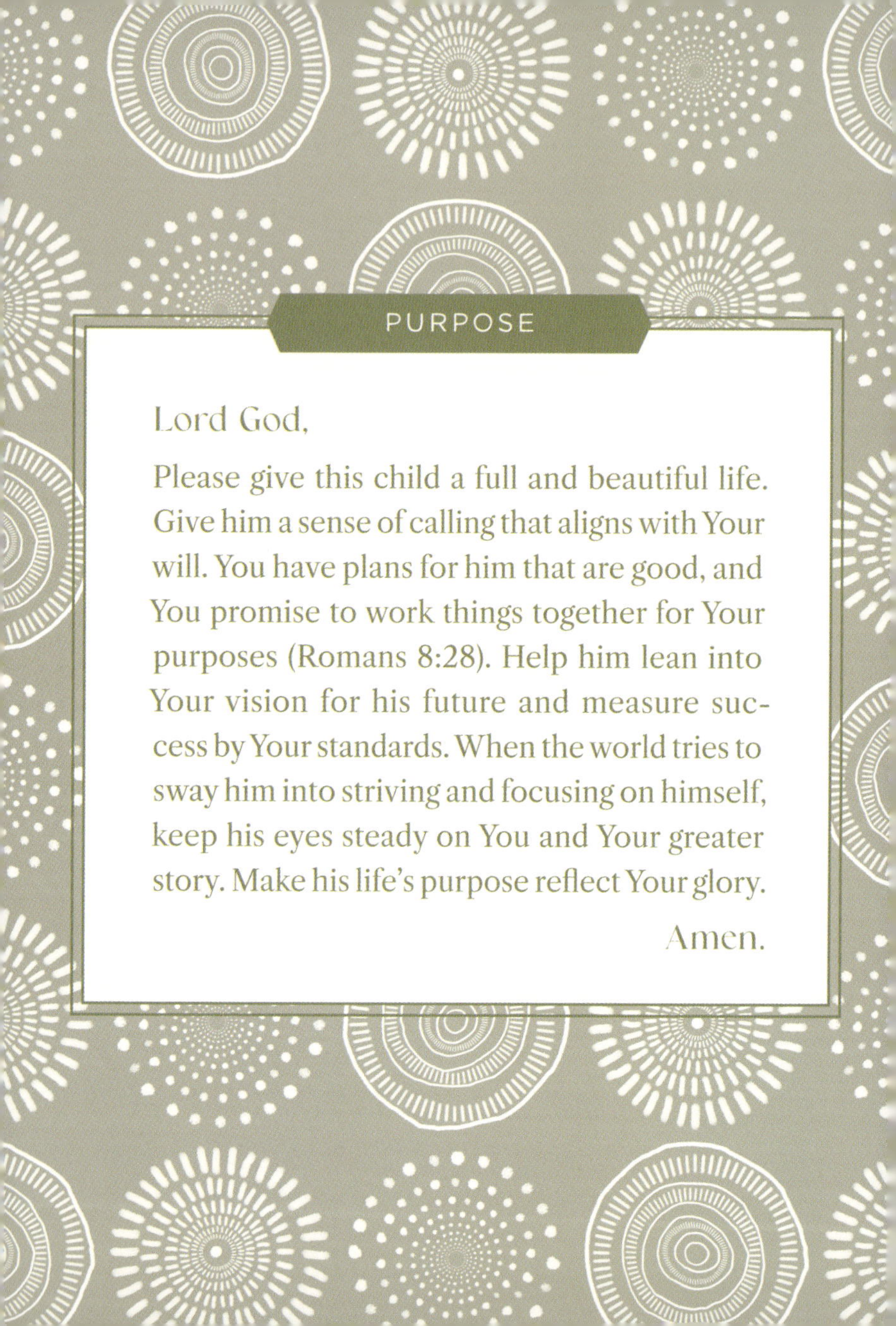

PURPOSE

Lord God,

Please give this child a full and beautiful life. Give him a sense of calling that aligns with Your will. You have plans for him that are good, and You promise to work things together for Your purposes (Romans 8:28). Help him lean into Your vision for his future and measure success by Your standards. When the world tries to sway him into striving and focusing on himself, keep his eyes steady on You and Your greater story. Make his life's purpose reflect Your glory.

Amen.

We know that God causes
everything to work together
for the good of those who love
God and are called according
to his purpose for them.

ROMANS 8:28

Not that I have already obtained this or am already perfect, but I press on to make it my own, because Christ Jesus has made me his own...One thing I do: forgetting what lies behind and straining forward to what lies ahead, I press on toward the goal for the prize of the upward call of God in Christ Jesus.

PHILIPPIANS 3:12-14 ESV

DETERMINATION

Dear God,

I want to believe that this little boy's life will be easy, but I know it will not always be so. Give him moments—even in the midst of struggle and discomfort and stretching and growth—where he is determined to strain forward to what lies ahead and seek the prize of whatever or wherever You call him (Philippians 3:12-14). Help him dig deep and find Your strength there, knowing that pushing forward into Your will is the safest and surest direction he can travel.

Amen.

FUTURE

Good Father,

I have dreams for this child, ones that include happiness and contentment with a family of his own one day. If that is Your will for him, Lord, please prepare a wife for him who is loving, kind, patient, compassionate, and, above all, a Jesus follower. If it is not Your plan for him to marry or have children, prepare for him a rich and wonderful life, filled to the brim with love and community. Whatever is in store for this child, prepare his heart to be loving and loved (Proverbs 16:9).

Amen.

We can make our
plans, but the LORD
determines our steps.

PROVERBS 16:9

I praise you, for I am fearfully
and wonderfully made.
Wonderful are your works;
my soul knows it very well.

PSALM 139:14 ESV

UNIQUENESS

Dear God,

I know too well that this precious baby boy was formed with precision by Your loving hand. You created him in Your image and love him exactly the way he's designed. Give him the soul-deep knowledge that he is worthy because he is fearfully and wonderfully made and Your work is always good (Psalm 139:14). Help him appreciate his uniqueness as a gift from You and use that knowledge to live a life of purpose to lead others to You.

Amen.

CREATIVITY

Dear God,

What wonderful things You have planned for this child throughout his life! Use his mind and hands and feet and creativity to bless the world with good works (Ephesians 2:10). Allow his eyes to see beyond the ordinary, ears to hear goodness, a mouth that praises, feet that serve, and an imagination open wide to everything You have in store for him. May his life leave a mark on humanity that reveals Your character and love.

Amen.

We are his workmanship, created
in Christ Jesus for good works,
which God prepared beforehand,
that we should walk in them.

EPHESIANS 2:10 ESV

Don't copy the behavior and customs of this world, but let God transform you into a new person by changing the way you think. Then you will learn to know God's will for you, which is good and pleasing and perfect.

ROMANS 12:2

DISCERNMENT

Dear God,

In a world that will constantly try to pull this child away from You, I ask that You give my son discernment so he can always hear Your good and perfect will. Sound alarms in his spirit to help him resist the temptations that are harmful, and illuminate the path of righteousness. Make him into a new creation, giving him clarity of mind, focus, and the desire to live a transformed life each and every day (Romans 12:2).

Amen.

PRAYER LIFE

Dear Heavenly Father,

I ask You to bless this boy's prayer life. Through all his days, call him to an ongoing, intimate, and meaningful conversation with You. Create a thread between Your heart and his, so he may feel the pull to be close to You. As he grows, tap him on the shoulder, whisper in his ear, sing to him. You promise if he comes to You in prayer and thanksgiving, Your peace will guard his heart and mind (Philippians 4:6-7). Lord, may Your voice be the one he always longs to hear.

Amen.

Don't worry about anything;
instead, pray about everything.
Tell God what you need, and
thank him for all he has done.
Then you will experience God's
peace, which exceeds anything
we can understand. His peace will
guard your hearts and minds
as you live in Christ Jesus.

PHILIPPIANS 4:6-7

Imitate God, therefore, in everything you do, because you are his dear children.

EPHESIANS 5:1

DESIRE TO BE LIKE JESUS

Dear God,

There will be so many people this baby boy admires throughout his life, and I hope I am one of them. But above all else, I want him to look up to You so he can imitate the best example of all. Give this child the desire to imitate Jesus and to love others because everyone is Your image bearer (Ephesians 5:1). By caring for others as You do, he will be a walking, talking messenger of Your love throughout the world. Help him see people and circumstances and the world with Your compassionate, loving eyes. May his heart beat in rhythm with Yours.

Amen.

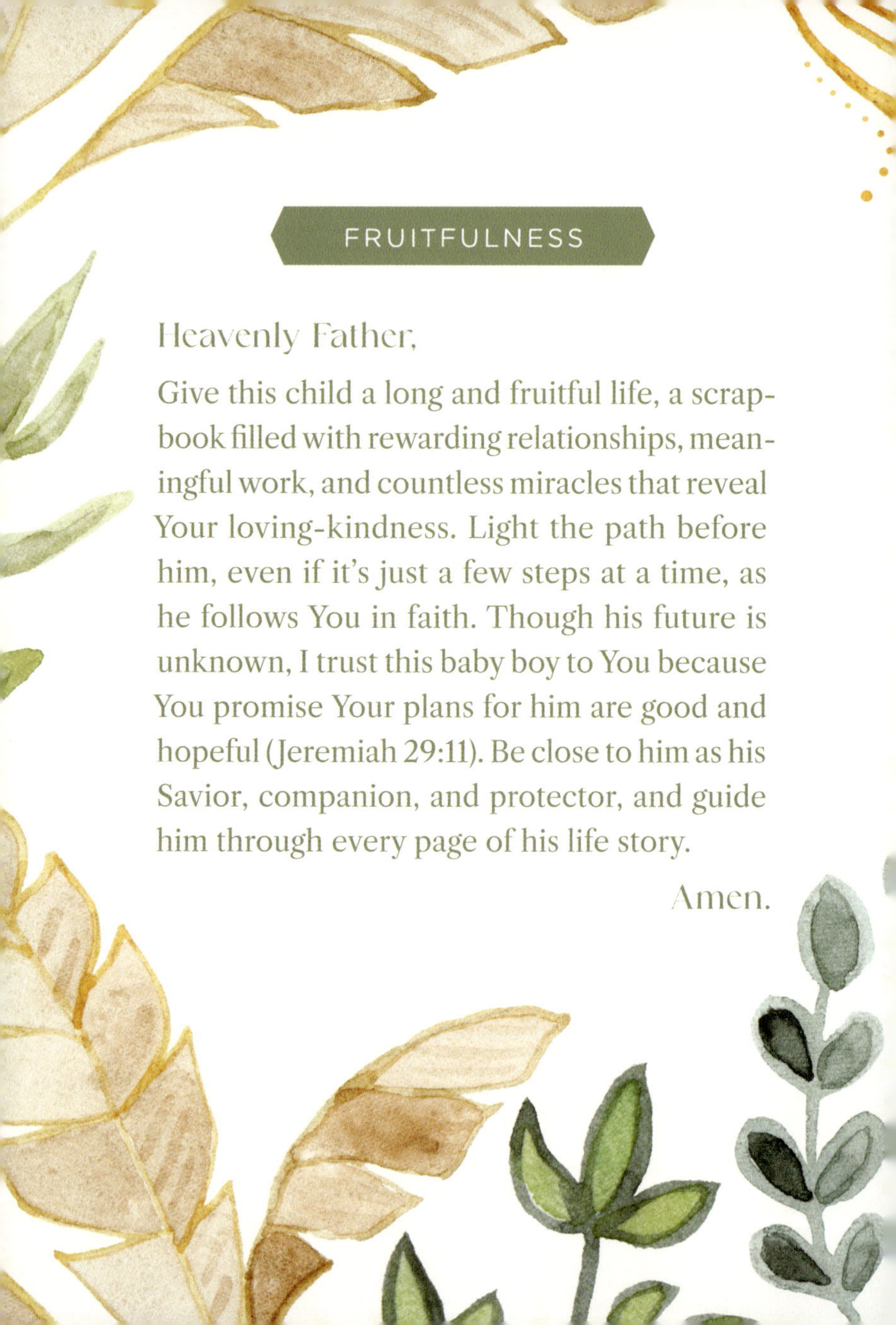

FRUITFULNESS

Heavenly Father,

Give this child a long and fruitful life, a scrapbook filled with rewarding relationships, meaningful work, and countless miracles that reveal Your loving-kindness. Light the path before him, even if it's just a few steps at a time, as he follows You in faith. Though his future is unknown, I trust this baby boy to You because You promise Your plans for him are good and hopeful (Jeremiah 29:11). Be close to him as his Savior, companion, and protector, and guide him through every page of his life story.

Amen.

"I know the plans I have for you," says the LORD. "They are plans for good and not for disaster, to give you a future and a hope."

JEREMIAH 29:11

All praise to God, the Father of our Lord Jesus Christ. God is our merciful Father and the source of all comfort. He comforts us in all our troubles so that we can comfort others. When they are troubled, we will be able to give them the same comfort God has given us.

2 CORINTHIANS 1:3-4

COMPASSION

Comforting Father,

How grateful I am to know You will comfort this child throughout his life. While I wish my child would never be troubled, I am thankful Your love and tenderness will allow him to learn how to comfort others—and he will be a blessing to those in similar circumstances (2 Corinthians 1:3-4). Help him to have a heart for those who need Your compassion, including himself. When it comes to generosity, may he be overflowing with compassion to others in need.

Amen.

HONESTY

Dear God,

Wrap honesty and integrity around this baby boy like a cloak. Allow these to be a source of warmth and strength throughout his life. Will You give him the desire to always speak the truth, no matter how difficult it might be? I know You want us to be honest not only when we pray to You but also in our every-day thoughts, words, and actions (2 Corinthians 8:21). Make his lips speak truth with love, and may his life be a living testimony as others watch and see Your goodness.

Amen.

We are careful to be honorable
before the Lord, but we also
want everyone else to see
that we are honorable.

2 CORINTHIANS 8:21

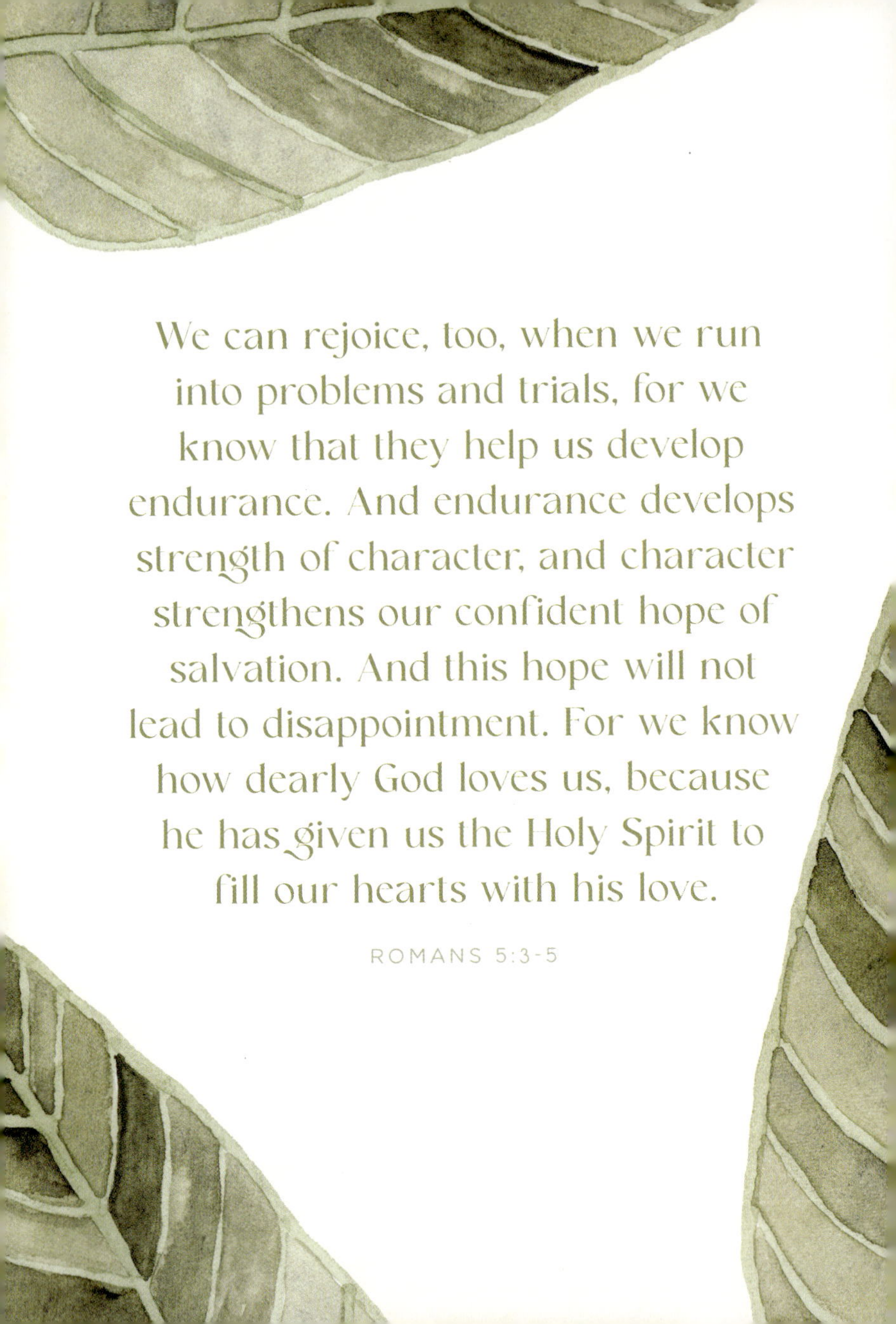

We can rejoice, too, when we run into problems and trials, for we know that they help us develop endurance. And endurance develops strength of character, and character strengthens our confident hope of salvation. And this hope will not lead to disappointment. For we know how dearly God loves us, because he has given us the Holy Spirit to fill our hearts with his love.

ROMANS 5:3-5

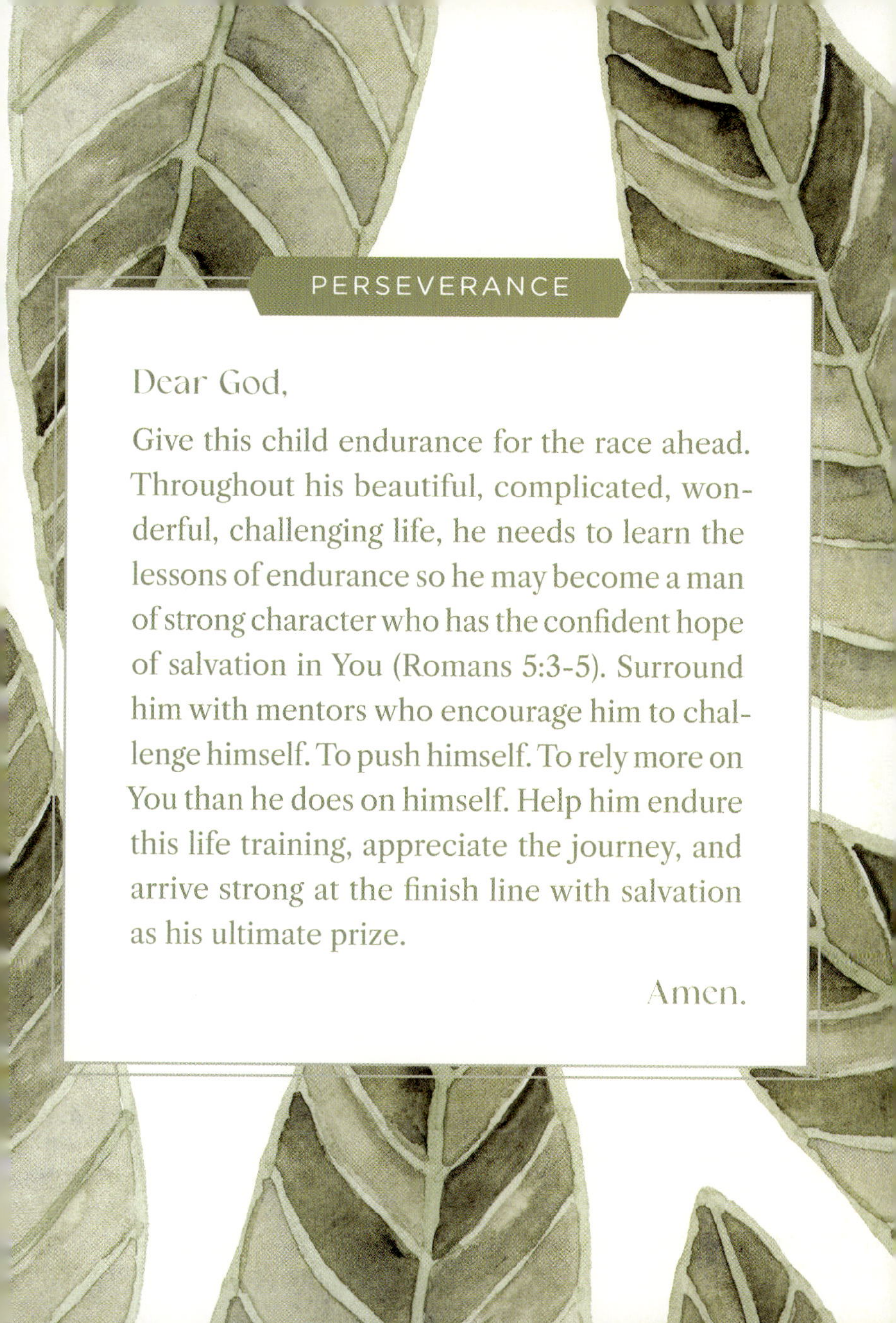

PERSEVERANCE

Dear God,

Give this child endurance for the race ahead. Throughout his beautiful, complicated, wonderful, challenging life, he needs to learn the lessons of endurance so he may become a man of strong character who has the confident hope of salvation in You (Romans 5:3-5). Surround him with mentors who encourage him to challenge himself. To push himself. To rely more on You than he does on himself. Help him endure this life training, appreciate the journey, and arrive strong at the finish line with salvation as his ultimate prize.

Amen.

FORGIVENESS

Forgiving Father,

I'm so thankful for Your forgiveness, and I know You sent Your Son to die on the cross for our sins. I ask that this baby boy learn the magnitude of Your gift at an early age and recognize the importance of forgiveness. As he learns this, please give him a compassionate heart that forgives others quickly and completely, knowing You require us to forgive others (Mark 11:25). Help me model this for him, and as he grows, may he become a beautiful example of Your sacrificial love for us.

Amen.

When you are praying,
first forgive anyone you
are holding a grudge against,
so that your Father in heaven
will forgive your sins, too.

MARK 11:25

O people, the LORD has
told you what is good, and
this is what he requires
of you: to do what is right,
to love mercy, and to walk
humbly with your God.
MICAH 6:8

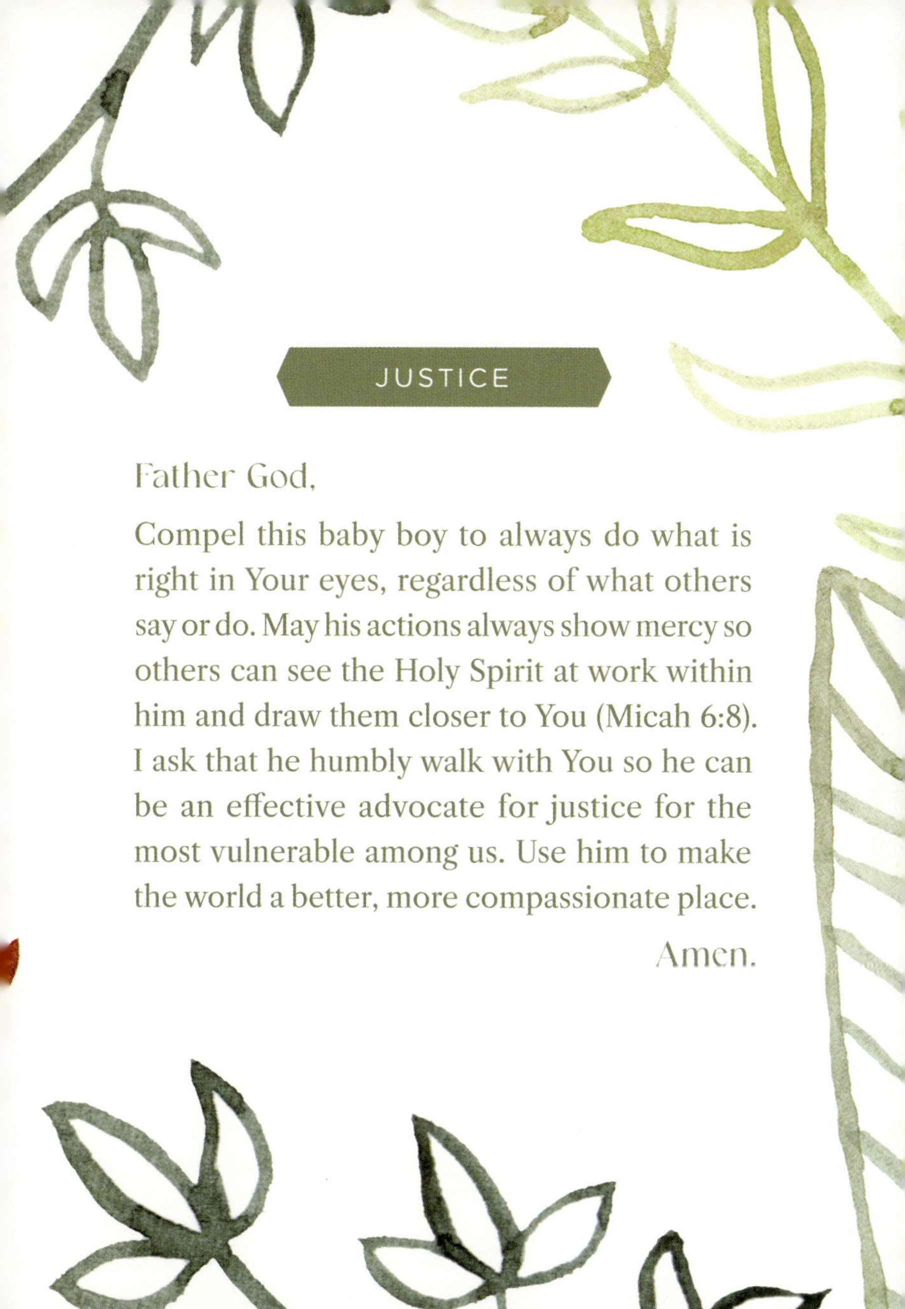

JUSTICE

Father God,

Compel this baby boy to always do what is right in Your eyes, regardless of what others say or do. May his actions always show mercy so others can see the Holy Spirit at work within him and draw them closer to You (Micah 6:8). I ask that he humbly walk with You so he can be an effective advocate for justice for the most vulnerable among us. Use him to make the world a better, more compassionate place.

Amen.

DELIGHT

Dear God,

Bless this boy with a lifetime of laughter and delight. Give him a spirit of joy, as a blessing not only to himself but to everyone around him. Have his lips be quick with a smile, a praise, a song, and uplifting words (Job 8:21) that will make others flock to him and his positivity. Allow him to be diligent in seeking out the good rather than focusing on the negative. Help him lead the way as others curiously follow his journey toward joy.

Amen.

[God] will once again fill your
mouth with laughter and
your lips with shouts of joy.

JOB 8:21

You will receive power when the Holy Spirit comes upon you. And you will be my witnesses, telling people about me everywhere—in Jerusalem, throughout Judea, in Samaria, and to the ends of the earth.

ACTS 1:8

BLESSING

Dear God,

I don't know the plans You have for this sweet child, but I know he is destined to be a blessing. To me, to others, and to You. Thank You for promising Your Holy Spirit to him when he accepts You as his Savior, and I ask that once he does, You would propel him into the world as a blessing wherever You lead him (Acts 1:8). Allow his testimony to impact every person he meets.

Amen.

HEALTHY BOUNDARIES

Dear God,

I ask that You'd instill healthy boundaries and a clear understanding of when to say yes and when to say no, according to Your will. Help him resist peer pressure, and give him a cheerful heart when he decides to give and a settled heart and mind when he doesn't (2 Corinthians 9:7). Whatever he seeks to do, remind him to pray for wisdom in all things, and help him hear Your strong, clear voice for direction.

Amen.

You must each decide in
your heart how much to give.
And don't give reluctantly
or in response to pressure.
"For God loves a person
who gives cheerfully."

2 CORINTHIANS 9:7

Everyone must submit to governing authorities. For all authority comes from God, and those in positions of authority have been placed there by God.

ROMANS 13:1

RESPECT FOR AUTHORITY

Dear God,

Thank You for the awesome privilege of guiding this child through his life. Prepare a heart within him that respects and honors authority, knowing that all authority ultimately comes from You, Lord (Romans 13:1). Help him seek Your will and guidance while also praying for those who are put in charge of leading him. Bless those who are put in the position of guiding this baby boy, providing him with wonderful mentors and friends who lead him closer and closer to You.

Amen.

Dear God,

Thank You for the bountiful array of emotions You have given this baby boy. As he grows in faith, allow the expressions of Your character to blossom and mature, exhibiting love, joy, peace, patience, kindness, goodness, faithfulness, gentleness, and self-control (Galatians 5:22-23). Use the Holy Spirit to radiate from him, giving him the ability to engage with others in a way that blesses him and them.

Amen.

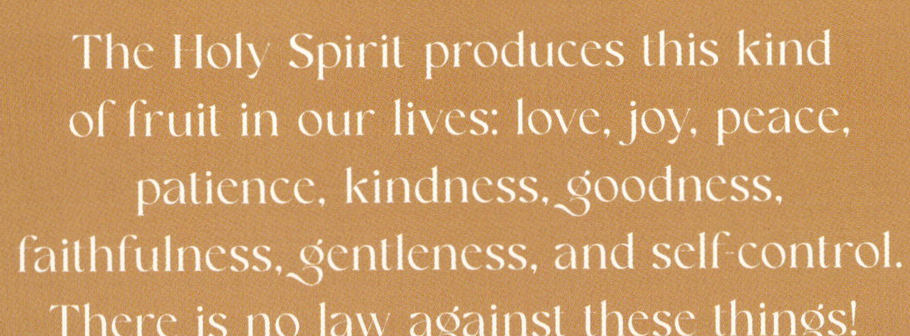

The Holy Spirit produces this kind of fruit in our lives: love, joy, peace, patience, kindness, goodness, faithfulness, gentleness, and self-control. There is no law against these things!

GALATIANS 5:22-23